QUARTET

Edited by/Herausgegeben von
Wilhelm Altmann

Ernst Eulenburg Ltd
London · Mainz · Madrid · New York · Paris · Tokyo · Toronto · Zürich

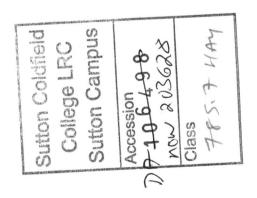

Quartet No 76

I

Joseph Haydn, Op. 76 No 2
1732 - 1809

E. E. 1110

4

II

Andante o più tosto allegretto

14

più adagio e più piano

E. E. 1110

III

Menuetto. Allegro ma non troppo.

18

M. D. C.

IV

26

E. E. 4410